# Strong John and the Hands of Antiquity

(Poems 2000–2003)

by Samana

Firewheel Editions

Cover: "Hand Over Bashō, on the Narrow Road to the Deep North" (Japanese Knotweed, *Falopia japonica*, Samana carved figure) Photo by Anna Bayles Arthur and Samana ©2010.

# Strong John and the Hands of Antiquity
(Poems 2000 – 2003)

## Contents

Reaches of Wildness and Thundering Water ................................................. 7
Hands ........................................................................................................ 11

### Part One

Break ........................................................................................................ 15
Look into My Eye ...................................................................................... 16
The Submission ......................................................................................... 17
Road Test .................................................................................................. 19
Strong John of the Deep Music ................................................................. 20
Design ...................................................................................................... 21
Will of God ............................................................................................... 22
The Model ................................................................................................ 23
The Beckoning Arm .................................................................................. 24
Community Oom ...................................................................................... 25
The Red Fox ............................................................................................. 26
A History of Jazz ....................................................................................... 28
A Beige Scarf ............................................................................................ 29
Train ......................................................................................................... 31
Hands of Antiquity on a Modern Face ...................................................... 32
Poem (It Came Out) ................................................................................. 33
The Incident. The Picnic ........................................................................... 34
In 500 Words or Less ................................................................................ 35
The Beetle ................................................................................................. 36
Hands Clapping ........................................................................................ 37
Before a Storm .......................................................................................... 39
Yellow Balloon Rising ............................................................................... 40
Death by Baloney ..................................................................................... 41
MRI .......................................................................................................... 43
Three Dresses Above Cripple Creek .......................................................... 44
Colors from the Attic ................................................................................ 45
Mother and Father .................................................................................... 46
Wolf Prose ................................................................................................ 47
Heart ........................................................................................................ 48
Superman ................................................................................................. 49
Death of a Thing ...................................................................................... 50

## Part Two

Dickinson ..................................................................53
Astronaut Family .........................................................54
Box for a Voice ...........................................................55
Forever Lyric ..............................................................56
Snowball, with Policeman ............................................57
The Man I Love ..........................................................58
Questioning Human Flight ...........................................59
The Diners .................................................................60
Darkness, ..................................................................61
Suicide ......................................................................62
Physicians .................................................................63
Dialogia .....................................................................64
Creature ....................................................................65
Anointed ...................................................................66
Crying Child ...............................................................67

## Part Three

Note to All Concerned .................................................71
Poem in Search of a Brother ........................................72
The Grape ..................................................................73
Field In July ................................................................74
The Murderer, the Murdered, and Me ..........................75
December 2002 Letter to My Friends ...........................76
Billy Should Have Swum Toward the Raft .....................78
Night in Haydenville ....................................................79
The Room ..................................................................80
More Questions for Study ............................................81
The Unintentional Thief ...............................................83
Walker .......................................................................84
Remnant ....................................................................85
Toyland .....................................................................86
The Lost Sock Being the One You Need .......................87
Hatfield .....................................................................88
You Be Time, I'll Be Fire ..............................................89
Fire ...........................................................................90
A Song ......................................................................92
Poem (Delicate Furniture) ...........................................93
The Lawn ..................................................................94
Euler Did Not Consider Case 2 ....................................97
Einstein .....................................................................99
Passengers ................................................................100

# Strong John and the Hands of Antiquity

(Poems 2000 – 2003)

This book is dedicated to Sacredlittle,
the great nun, student and attendant.

# Reaches of Wildness and Thundering Water

Dear Reader,

     Very pleased to have you hold *Strong John and the Hands of Antiquity* in your hands. Very aware, too, that many poets do not get to type that sentence.

     Samana thinks about all the vegetables that he is able to channel to people who need them. Organic kale, chard, collards, dandelion greens, and every kind of lettuce; cucumbers, zucchini, spinach, basil, and fennel; beets, radishes, corn, parsley; and this is the part of the sentence where the reader can add anything grown in the Connecticut River Valley. All of it this Monk, Samana, and his attendant, Sacredlittle, find at the local farmers' markets, on Saturdays and Tuesdays, here in Northampton, and together the two of us wheel three or four shopping carts full of freshly harvested produce down to the public housing where we live. By the end of the day, with the collaboration of nine or so farmers and people who need, approximately 150 people are fed wholesome food from local farms. Samana would be remiss not to mention bread which we pick up weekly from four bakeries in Northampton, bringing it also to people who cannot afford healthy, organic loaves. People can't live by bread alone, true, yet they need the bread along with the fresh greens.

     A writer is a person voluntarily pushing a full cart from the farm to the people. Sexuality, gender, slavery, race, and history; ostracism, family abuse and trauma, a planet crying out for change; the beauty of love, and the terrible beauty when your heart really breaks: these are some of the wares that this farmer has found growing on the land. These are not things planted in rows; not steady lines measured in feet; no raised beds of stanzas or quatrains. And yet there is form here, a permaculture of form, where great nut-bearing trees rise up, and there is enough water, sun, and cool shade for berry bushes beneath. This book the very garden and the farm of a body saying what it had to say, one day after another, one day to the next. Three years of this physical and spiritual practice, and the manuscript channeled from this core of being exists.

Exists, lives, first as a 170-page manuscript, poems from 2000-2003. Then a slower work, by other pruning hands, begins. The hands are those of the same body, yet on another day, another man. This writer on this page is not even him; this writer is the one who makes the letter to the reader. That writer sits between this one and the one who originally channeled the poems. Each day, coming as editor, philosopher, social critic, son and lover, the rereader and rewriter comes to the page as a more slowly moving animal. He seeks to read, to understand, to fathom the healthful movement of the land. How well do these two or three or five plants grow together? Might this be pruned and that expanded, given more room to range and/or grow? And where, also, to leave and to respect reaches of wildness and thundering water? What ecosystems, perhaps initially unseen or still mysteriously unknown, need not to be destroyed by a patriarchal or managerial hand? And is this book a manifestation of grace? Does it care? Does it act as love? Can it serve?

There are cars, vehicles, rockets, and bombs in this book, yet the writer of it has neither been in a car nor left Northampton for years. This is part of Samana's permanent Vow of Stability, never again in this life to travel by car, bus, train, or plane. Don't look for him at a bookstore or college near you. Not travelling is part of this monk's committed relationship to a planet that is calling for the action of political change. And a poem is a relationship a person has with the resources that happen to be in the day. Not different than the relationship one has with vegetables and bread, with money, children, or time. A poem as a way of focusing, committing, and spending one's limited being.

The writer of this book has only his face through which to see the world. Yet he sees the world through many who grow inside him, who inhabit, who have houses and farms of their own within. And he feels the hands of the ages, as well as the work of generations to come, mapping their knowing hands over his mortal face.

Samana<br>
for the Sanctuary<br>
July 2010, Northampton

*The root of the word shaman, Samana means Monk. From the Sanskrit, Samana also means to breathe equally, or equal breath. It is the body's breath that has to do with absorption and assimilation. In July 2010, Samana took his final vows as a monk and founding member of the Northampton Group, and his attendant, Sacredlittle, took her final vows as a nun. A monk, a nun, and a handful of students, we are on our way, a continuation of a story already in progress. Write to us if you'd like. Box 321, Northampton, MA 01061.*

# Hands

The left, three times in my life, partially inside someone else's spouse.

I am not a doctor poet and don't condemn me.

The boy blames the father who brought him to live in fire.

Until a moment ago, say fifteen years, I would have beaten the light out of a boy who beat his dog.

You'll note that the circle of rage need not contain a second body.

If I could get my hands on myself, I would kill him. Some people do that,

that's what it's like to have a body that is a neighboring city.

If we lived in bottles, bobbed around in the sea, and had space and distance between us—but that's not practical, we have yet to define the problem.

Can you trust the hand that is holding the page?

Spider in the corner of the web, the way it stands on its nerves, admirable architecture.

Beautiful is not in the mind of the fly in the web, it has taken a vow of stability for the rest of its life,

it pays the rent with its vibrating body, it hums and helps to build its own Taj Mahal.

My right is not the tail of the dinosaur, the intelligent left sports the brain.

If they applaud you, it's from a covert desire to strike one another, small animals that they are, coy girls.

Habits: to bring oblivion to the face, to come together for safety, cop a feel, get laid, pray.

# Part One

# Break

Beneath this poem, there is a break in the plaster.

Fighting with my girlfriend, I punched a hole in the wall.

Afterward, I pushed her small body into the hole.

She settled in, her delicate ribs lightly and safely between the dependable ribs of wood.

She hunted at night, she always had owl-like eyes.

I could hear the death cries of small rats and mice, she harpooned them with her pen or hairpin.

There are many ways to build a poem, a life, she rubbed together two angry teeth, hummed while she cooked prey over her fire in the wall.

When she slept on her side, I touched the mound of plaster that was her hip.

On her back, I read the features of her face, breasts, knee, lovely feet.

Magpies pile up on the phone machine, the lie of her voice, it claims to be her.

She swims in the water underneath the poem, every page hides a hole in a wall.

# Look into My Eye

There you will find another of the world's tiny forests.

My mother sits in her kitchen chair at the base of a pine tree.

Needles tick when they spring from the trees,
pine cones make a cushioned bump when they hit the brown needle floor.

You'd have to listen to hear this,

you would have to be not my mother, who is unaware of the clouds.

They gather and muscle, they spit at the people on the horizon.

My mother is no callous woman,
she cares for people who suffer in other countries,

yet here in my eye we have only her, the tree, her chair of grief and the lake toward which she leans.

A painter would make her ear large, or blue, hang from the lobe an earring,

small sphere on which a boy circles on his bicycle, totters and does not fall.

She cannot see the lake, the trees have taken years to assume a formation to block her view,
the lap of water on stones, she can feel that in her heart.

And, with a murmured thud, men there are beating a fish against a stone.

This has gone on for all time, and she wonders in her heart

whether there is another way to put down a fish, her son.

The boy on a small globe, singing from her ear, still circles on a bicycle.
Pine needles ping, they fling themselves free.

I weep for my murdered brother, her son, the fish and the inevitable men.

# The Submission

I'm an imbecile.

Wanting to send out poems, I begin by walking in the opposite direction.

The men in the park pass their unholy brown paper bag.

Each mentally calculates how long each of the others pulls on the upturned bottle.

Only other liberal imbeciles like me expect wisdom from them.

Yet, they are wise to a thing or two. Their expectations do not exceed the contents of the bag.

I wake to the clock, disgusting news. Having wet my hair, I drink tea.

I find clothes from last night where I had dropped them.

Suddenly I'm outside, wearing the same ideas, carrying in my hand the submission.

I am not in a villa in the south of Italy.

I'm in a city, filthy because of the fourth week of a garbage strike.

If all of us stopped showering, we could come to realize that we are animals.

I read the newspaper, how disgraceful we were yesterday, and are expected to be tomorrow.

Writing in the margins, I am at work on the submission.

I'm not growing food, which involves turning the soil, inadvertently cutting worms in half with my spade.

I'm not delivering a baby, who may grow up to be a ruthless dictator, an astronaut, or a ballerina.

Scribbling like thousands of other imbeciles, I'm obsessed with the thought that I am unique and important.

Despite the idea of my bloated worth, the men in the park allow me into their circle.

They stare at one another's shoes, the subdued enthusiasm taught to them by other days like this one.

They maintain a tolerant silence while I read the submission.

## Road Test

Can anybody tell me what a road is?

A road is a place where you put your eyeglasses, sir.

Respondent one, that's a fine, last waking act before sleep.

Civil engineers are children who've never grown up: a road is a line shot like a dart through an enormous field so that later they can admire it from a helicopter in the sky.

Someone give that person a foil-wrapped kiss.

The Brooklyn Bridge is a short hair that fell from the sky where two giants were making love on a couch in 1923.

But is the turtle courageous, the moon pulling her across?

Which says nothing about the punk rocker who safety-pins a chicken's beak to his leather,

or the eggs that hatch, and one day will have to cross back.

The crow eats a fishhead, accustomed to you at sixty-five miles and hour.

The bird's awkward philosophy and the stitches that connect us;

the modern soul and the roadkill.

# Strong John of the Deep Music

Gods dip their warm breads in fine oil, watching over the green tea and espresso of our lives.

Each month a smaller lump in your throat, still you are not eager to kick grief out of the lonely house.

It is as they say: Loss sings no more poorly than any other guest come to look over the birthday cake.

And the explosions in the schoolyard of memory occur, regardless of what dinner, or how well the floor is scrubbed.

Confluence of apparent disparities only appears to be more of a shame—while we use the dustpan to gather up the glass, and have to skirt the broad colorful ribbons, the buoyant helium balls of celebration.

All of this to say: I wish you were here, and that you didn't have to be.

Remember that you can't stop the Dalai Lama from gazing brokenly at the surface of the deep lake.

Where is the hammer, when one needs to drive nails through a board, in the place that once boasted a window, admitted light?

The same window, would you say, in an effort to develop the plot, begin or enhance a theme, through which the man who stood in the garden, a briefcase with a trenchcoat, once stared while you stepped from the shower, your arms overhead drying hair?

Strong John of the Deep Music only now begins to tune his guitar, to compose a little something that will do justice to the tin of our everyday light, while not excluding the odd angel, the gargoyle hanging over the boulevard.

Saints from the desert of the second century step one by one from the lyrics that he is putting down. Soft tears, they save your life.

It's as the ancients told us: Be quiet now.

# Design

Two words joined together are a harbor for grief.

The harbor casts a shadow, fish beat beneath in the cold.

We lip the water: air, food, shafts of light.

Barnacles hug the wood piling, pore to pore,
the tide and the sun conspire.

With the morning, a delivery of new recruits.

A baby is born with a mouth that knows
the warmth and rumble of mother, punch of a lung as it fills and flattens,

and ears remember the father's voice from before.

Homogenous humanity, prison of curved ribs, fluidity of earliest existence,
knowledge of the dark, warm delta.

# Will of God

A balloon reaching for the altitude at which explosions occur. An aerial photograph of a field taken by brush fire. The pollen, a spore from Texas, which genetically alters corn in Mexico. Potatoes planted in steps on the sunny side of a cold mountain. A person inside a drum, in a room beneath the bass report of footsteps, the talking of God. The thunder, the lightning, the face lit for a second and is gone. The face followed by another face, the faces in a crowd, they bleed, they weep. The history of faces, their relationship to boots, to razor wire. The thud thud of boots, of faces being delivered to fire. The razor a man drags across his face successfully avoiding his eyes. The drapes behind which mother died. The eyes of poor Oedipus, first one then the other. Tremendous accomplishments, Father hanging himself from a beam in the barn. Mother's clothesline cut in two, the question of what to do with the other half. Overcooked meat, uncooked meat, the living cow, whether to eat the cloned cattle. Each chicken protected from each chicken, the millions of chickens without beaks. A heat-seeking missile. A one-hundred-percent artificial heart.

# The Model

She takes a break, puts on her robe.

Lighting the stove, I give her tea.
Mint in the garden, May rain. In her face, a touch of ash.

I pull a tear out of the corner of my eye, the model says physiological.

Doesn't she ever feel unsafe, posing this way for strangers?

I've got an axe in that bag, she says, pointing to her backpack, and she laughs.

She stands, comfortable again in my studio, her nipples are eyes.
With her belly they make a face, a small animal beneath.

I'm not being stupid, this is not a hunger for me,

but lips by nature are hungry.

Something like worry shows on the model's face, then is gone.

Later together, on the path back toward town, she takes my arm,

a dead starling poses beneath the giant chestnuts in blossom.

# The Beckoning Arm

When a dog walks by your house and you're sleeping, your father in sunlight leans against a tall fence.

The fire wants outside the window, wants to burn its way out of your sleeping house.

Two dogs pass together, in sleep there's a violence of shadows. The limbs fly.

The dead arm is a fatal question. Does it belong to the man who used it to prop up his head after making love to his wife for how many nights?

Is the arm the property of the man who took it, and does it matter on which side of the fence it falls?

My grandmother clothed her grief in black cotton, a cross, and how is it with the arm? Could it be the property of the dogs that signify?

Do righteousness and evil have anything to say about the integrity and ownership of the solitary, quivering hand?

And what about the fingers twisted into roots for the picture in sunlight, the elbow a whitecap or mountaintop?

Or is the arm property only of itself and the distances,

does it belong to the gorgeous river moving from what had been the shoulder,

something in all the red trying to get to where we are, and to tell us?

# Community Oom

Numerous uniformed men are in a circular birdcage.

I fear that I have gotten further away from the road you walk on.

This is the place that my horse froze to death in a previous life.

Karma: my parents return as wolverines chased by tigers.

And a wolverine is not an easy animal.

Listen, those must be jackals, they promise a conclusion.

Centurions in dresses surround my heart, they fire their arrows. The Emperor learns I have survived it. He sends the centurions to club me to death. This piece is written in the space before they return.

There is consolation: being fired upon in a cage together.

Off to one side, Oedipus chats with Timothy McVeigh.

Lots of jokes: in the hallways, on the elevator, at the mailboxes, in the Community Oom.

The R fell off the door long ago.

Laughter comes from deep in their throats, they are discussing the military.

A hill does not pass us by. It approaches, it covers, it plans to stay.

Oedipus and McVeigh asked me to tell you they are not ashamed of us.

The sun thinks this is all very funny.

Do you doubt this?

I refer you to drawings made by children.

# The Red Fox

A summary, then, of your early life?

Not exactly. I am a cartoon pussycat. My father the bulldog drives me into the earth. A stake.

This is done with a mallet?

With a fist that becomes a mallet. I stay put.

Like a dream.

Nothing is like anything. Remember, you were a child once.

The fist is a mallet. Malleable.

You know, I was thinking yesterday. I don't have much hair. Still my head is a beautiful orange.

Of course there's that poem, in your fifth unpublished volume. Your mother made hats.

It was her way to get inside my father. Once there she arranged the furniture. Put the fireplace where the icebox had been.

The story you tell, in *Recipes*.

He reaches in for an evening snack. Pulls out a handful of glowing embers, tosses them down his throat, then goes to look in on his child. She's dying in her small bed. He speaks over her, the nastiest words in the language. We all know what they are. Before she can get out of the woods in her dream, where she is being pursued by the Red Fox, the child is on fire. Her bedclothes, the mattress, become a symphony around her. I will always remember my little sister on a page surrounded by musical notation.

"The Mercy, for a child who goes in her sleep./ She rests beneath a ladder still."

We have to be careful there. Torres-Táma comes from a line of housepainters. His father, his father's father. Even his great-grandfather.

So we're working here with a literal ladder—

We learn to be less dependent on words.

The object runs away, when you pick up your hammer.

Exactly. Some of my first-year students have trouble with that.

Over the years, you've been shot more than a dozen times, in one or another of your workshops.

"If you've been shot once, you've been shot a thousand times." (Laughs) My mother was a peasant, you know.

Would you elaborate on that?

No.

But this is an interview.

But I'm bigger than you are. And there's something desperate in the way I give the baby her bottle.

But I'll have to start all over—if you take my friends from me.

No one can hear you. You are a man in a large, treeless field, a rope around your neck. You hold the end in your hands. You pull, first one way, then the other.

What the hell I'm doing that for?

It's the book you were born into.

I turn the page.

The glue on the binding already dried before you were a turtle in your mother's womb.

I see her in a field. She's knitting a rope out of her own hair. It's my mother.

You begin your story with what fills your hands.

# A History of Jazz

There once was a woman who wanted to learn Jazz.

A man who would be her teacher came with his friends and got her.

He beat her, raped her, set her to work, tied her to a post outside the barn. Inside standing horses whinnied in their sleep.

The man sat and became a really fat fuck, while, for one who died young,

she done had a load of babies,
didn't get but to name a few, kept just the one.

It took a few centuries for the man's neighbors to complain.

And then the woman came back for her great grandkids, flying outside their windows,

laying on them the gift of a language.

# A Beige Scarf

I am an ordinary man. Checking my attic you find

hundreds of bales of tissue paper, each one containing 24 rolls,

cans of waxed beans, beets, crushed tomatoes, in an unknown number,
ten sacks each of brown and white rice, ten pounds to the sack,

and in burlap eight, 25-pound sacks of dry beans, pinto, black, navy.

There's something you're forgetting, a beige scarf that your mother wore.

I thought that those were branches, thin leaves growing out like forks.
Later I discerned each small eye, the sinew, river-like curve of a snake.

When she wasn't at home?

I took the scarf down from the wooden peg beside the door,
placed it on the floor.

You always knew when she would not return soon,
the brush with gray bristles, the brown soap, the pail and the rag
    were gone.

And beneath the sink, the pipe drips *plink* into a can that once held fruit.

A man I saw only in heavy sleep, his face in the clouds,
had left behind a pair of rotten boots, mud and snow had worn and
    curved them.

The boots had no color, their laces held together bundles of twigs by
    the stove.

If pushed, you would say that the color was green.

The boots were green. I wore them to my shins, my feet were small
    children
in a large clay pot, language walking over the scarf of snakes.

It was wise to stop when your shins began to bleed.

The scars grew long, as my body lengthened.

When you lie in bed, it is summer, your lover traces the sensitive skin with her tongue.

# Train

A train moved on the horizon, a woman crossed and uncrossed her legs.

Trees flew by outside her window.

A man stood in the darkness, watching a train move on the horizon.

Her scent, she breathed. She crossed and uncrossed her legs. Tress flew by.

As far as the night could tell. A man stood on the horizon. Beneath a tree.

She crossed and uncrossed her legs. She breathed her scent. Trees flew by. In a train on the horizon. She breathed.

A man stood in the dark, a train flew by. As far as the night could tell.

They were close. He was nearly inside her. Her scent. She breathed. He stood. A train flew by. The trees.

As far as the night could tell. There was no distance between them. She crossed and uncrossed her legs.

He breathed. She is inside him. On a train on the horizon. Trees fly by. She crosses and uncrosses her legs.

Her scent.

# Hands of Antiquity on a Modern Face

I meet Oedipus on the road between countries.

My most unpopular view was my body, he tells me.

We pause. It's a crossroads. There are gods, we feed them corn,
Oedipus is careful.

I'm impolite. I stare into his twitching face.

There are things I lack, whatever it takes to ask him about Antigone,

I wonder if he had a dog, a favorite, that licked his hands, that face.

I understand the first eye, but what is it to take the second?

A definition of myth: as big as you are.

His mother and his wife killed herself.
It ran in the family, his half-sister and his daughter did the same thing.

He wants me closer, I'm afraid for my neck.

He maps his hands over my forehead, my face.

I wanted to know

who you are.

# Poem (It Came Out)

It came out like a true vein, the thing
the junkie thinks will last forever,

the longest worm you've ever seen,

10,000 ants in a column, each contributing a *Yes*
to the rest of the relatives.

How it can be, the way a bird flies, through a puzzle of twigs.

How many miles an hour, I can't say. Ignorance an echo of my respect.

Lifting, dipping, brother.

Annihilating himself, on my window at dusk.

# The Incident. The Picnic.

They took hundreds of us out to the woods, divided us into camps.

In what seemed random, some were beaten.

Some filled out questionnaires, received stipends, treated to a catered dinner,
liquor, dancing, and the patriotic songs.

A boy vanished. Another was apprehended, sentenced to be a fruit in a box.

It happened, a number of the women, saying that they had said *No*.

In the cities, not so much outcry as general confusion, watching the tv news.

There were queers among us, artists known to create things, a child with a book,
many whose phones died beneath the trees.

The governor's wife, hinting she might run, called it *The Incident. The Picnic.*

Investigative teams recommended the state house sculpture, a gray, iron mound.

The anniversary, declared a holiday, the festival to be held in the woods.

Some will protest. We all plan to go.

# In 500 Words or Less

In the original *Wizard of Oz,* does the dog gain something when he discovers the man behind the curtain?

Compare an incident in your life to the moment in *1984* when the cage with the rat is strapped onto Winston Smith's head.

If all the fish swim upstream to die there, does it matter that they do it together? (Explain your use of *together*.)

Running with her fingernails into the vestibule, a woman is shouting. What's that beneath her nails?

Thinking: enormous boxcars stuffed with fresh fruit.

Lovely legs, says the man in a suit. He fingers a sheet of prose.

If you don't think it's work, join the circle in the park where they pass the bag.

Spend a year in prison instead of the Peace Corps, and I'll read the book.

When we were young, there was a booth. We threw balls at a painted face.

Please say it isn't so.

# The Beetle

No one should have to die like that, on his back on my kitchen floor.

Everyone related to someone somehow,

I pay the rent, my light draws him in from the dark.

A dry, stained coffee cup from goodwill,
cover it with a magazine, our lines of terror and experiment.

This is the beetle's peculiar, new ship.

A temporary, dark passage, a small death, a crypt.

No use dumping him on the carpet in the hall,
apartment building spiders would eat him alive.

Undergraduate combat boots, crushing his kin after last call.

The floodlights at the back of the building, away
from the moths, and the mosquitoes, circles of night combat.

Is he a he, or is she a she?
This beetle.

Free in a field, a half-moon, the clouds playing bumper cars.

Beware the dawn, the workmen at the college,
with their brown paper bags, their meat sandwiches.

They put up the small yellow flags, warning us, our children and pets,
spelling death for your kind.

# Hands Clapping

Of the half dozen Jazz concerts Mary Jo had seen, one had been recorded. She had a copy of it. Those were her hands coming together after each set.

She had sat at Table 5, had had the gardenburger, while the band unpacked its weariness from behind the smoky glass windows of the bus.

If you arrived early, you didn't have to sit behind a post.

That's where he had sat. She had felt his eyes on her, her black skirt, loose white blouse, hair pulled and tied to frame her porcelain face.

She didn't hate the sun. She liked to wear her big hat downtown, an awning to look out from. She could see the world better from her porch.

She had worn no underwear. The large fans in the club would push around the excessive heat.

She had used scent on her body. It had all come up at the trial.

They had asked about the previous night. She told no one of the dream of being hunted by her father.

She awoke with the image of her head on the wall.

Following necessary coffee and the terrible newspaper, which she put down unread for the cat, she touched herself in the shower not only to be clean.

Mary Jo listened to her hands clapping on the recording.

Had anyone else who'd been there that night gone to the store to buy the music?

Many who clapped beside her would appear in court. Wolf whistles, screams, animal yells.

Among them a man who would testify he had seen her and the defendant together near the restrooms.

She had peed. She was a generous tipper. She had asked the waitress to guard her prize table up front.

Perhaps she would share it?

In any recording of the evening, she does not make it home alone.

# Before a Storm

Without getting up from the table, without ever leaving your chair,

you walked out the door
into the air that is always there just before a storm,

always there anytime two people are sharing a meal,

only you weren't sharing a meal, you had the two
token things on your plate—spoon of rice, spoon of greens—

sitting there not eating and not speaking
as a way of saying something

about suffering, yours and mine, the one you felt
you had every right to, and the other one you were causing,

sitting there, too, with your half-glass of calories,
pausing over the red wine

to muse out loud between a beer or whiskey for dessert,

and settling for the shot over ice, which made me look twice
at my wrist, where I don't wear

and have never worn a watch, saying it was my time to fly,

into the air always thick with crows before a storm.

# Yellow Balloon Rising

The overflowed tub leaves a moon grimace on the far wall of the pantry,

a yellow balloon. It's President Nixon's unsmiling crayon face
come back to rise toward the offending bather.

In heaven, Princess Di sponges herself and tries to forget the thousands without legs.

A hawk circles for the seven-year-old boy I was.

My backyard, swaying trees toss sap on my mother, perennial flower,

who stands at a kitchen sink four-hundred miles south of here.

Trumpeting, an elephant who is my father,
a truck floating diesel over my lemonade, my summer.

Clouds like these have parted, many religious people have ascended.
Bushes have spoken, lightning has written words into stone.

Why should the book of my life go without ruby slippers?

Why should you not be carried away by flying monkeys?

# Death by Baloney

*for Lloyd*

Why do you think the author calls this poem "Death by Baloney"? Would the title "Death by Chicken" have made you think other things? Explain.

The language in "Death by Baloney" is straight forward. What makes this a poem? If you think this is not a poem, go and get a drink of water from the fountain.

A simple Yes or No will do. Do you like baloney?

Do you think that you would like this author if you met him?

Has your school merged history/humanities/English into one department?

Are you studying engineering? Is this one of those requirements that you must complete? Discuss what you intend to 'engineer' in the world.

If you liked the author, has that changed?

Can you know anyone if you don't know yourself?

And what does it mean to believe in anything?

When I was a boy, I watched from across the Hudson while the Twin Towers were being built, and my voice changed. "Baloney," I said, with new, sonorous integrity, hating, with most adults there, this new, unnatural symbol that had come to replace the lone cock of the Empire State Building, the tallest building in our souls. A kind of unbaloney.

I have always been a child in a rowboat on the tense surface of language.

Pair up, compare answers with the person to your left. Consider that there are 2 million prisoners in the US. A large percentage of them are descended from slaves. What relevance does this poem have a) to them? b) to you? Include in your answer your race. Listen to the sound of your voice.

Have you ever been in prison? What did you eat?

"All rice is cheap," the author is quoting himself as having said when asked in an interview about this poem, adding "if you've got a twenty-five pound bag in your cupboard."

What the hell could that possibly mean?

Who is Lloyd? Do you want to meet him? What are you most afraid of?

For extra credit, cry.

Go out and eat some rice, or some baloney. Has your relationship with either changed? Your associations? Rice,

baloney. A child floats, reading the bottom of the lake.

# MRI

The angel carpenters bang and scrape with their hammers and their saws.

We slice and make resonant images in order to find.

My brain is the heaven of this apprenticeship.

Imagine them young, novice angels sent to slice and photograph.

See how they sit on the scaffolding between images,
they joke over their boxed lunches.

How many sparrows, one can't count, bold on the wire of science.

Red and white cars stream below, something is bumper to bumper.

The midnight land within, a community of ants.

Neurons bomb a portion of my brain.

In this section a pink pig is being chased by dogs.

The next sliver is a photo of my old backyard, all cement,
a lawn chair upturned, its legs working in the sun.

A silver, 1950s' print of the smoke exhaled from the nostrils of my mother.

There is no privacy in the dark room of everything I've done.

Military command authorities surround Dr. John O'Connell's receptionist at her computer.

"Look," says Sandy, bringing up an image. "While here in our waiting room, how he lingered over the ads in the women's magazines."

The angels are eating the baloney sandwiches packed by God, roasted red pepper, artichoke heart.

They are drinking from goblets the lemonade of my youth.

# Three Dresses Above Cripple Creek

She would wear the one dress, he would carry the other two in the box from the store.

Any plan could contain their necessary heat.

He whistled under the dripping oaks. In puddles she looked up her dress.

Their fixed place was the field beyond the ravine.

While he ate dinner, corn on the cob had a particular sweetness,

her raspberry tart with that sharp tang.

Guests at their houses read preoccupation into their faces. Nobody much likes a thing he doesn't understand.

He splashed shaving water, she used her mother's cream.

Together they had shopped for the three new dresses.

The clerk had watched while the girl had tried on for the boy.

He had taken the afternoon off from the pit.

They took off each dress in its turn, the moon breathing over the puddles.

A great thing sank into the lake.

It is a legend Lester the firefighter will tell.

How they burned the girl behind the barn in her yellow dress.

How the boy tipped from his rowboat.

How the ghost of an oar can be heard cracking the new moon.

# Colors from the Attic

When it rains, the house cries onto the silver print of Grandfather.

It weeps onto the yellow hair of a sister's doll, washes over the fire truck, the real bronze bell.

The swing where we played lives on one rusted chain, its laughter waxes the stairs in the hall.

In the center of the bedroom hangs the single blue ball that is the doll's remaining eye. You must walk around it every day.

It rains without stopping, from room to room, the colors from the attic collect,

each to a bucket, each a particular note or phrase.

Tomorrow we expect the trombones of snow, the dark wall that is a father's voice.

# Mother and Father

Each of you has a body at your door, I say.

They nod. *A body is good furniture.*

*A place to look back from*, adds the other.

*When we were young, we were separate bodies. Nothing was one kind.*
*A falling off without a center.*

My father, looking down at his feet, how he wishes he were wearing his shoes.

*I was small, but never a boy. I had my own key to the quiet house.*

Something at the window has caught my mother's eye. Blood on a sparrow.
Her stare seems thirty years younger.

*There was one small room in our flat no one could go into*, she says.

Smoke from her cigarette, a thousand rivers in her eye, the bird stopping there
to pull one red twig free.

My father clears the knife from his throat. He sounds like a young bear.

*There will be time, there will be spaghetti. Coffee in the morning.*

*You, too, will grow old.*

# Wolf Prose

I return home to entertainment, already their coats are dry kindling, the house damp with musk, I smell that they have been breeding. Rude fur, watery tongues, eyes that I keep falling into. This is a conversation without a finding, an agreement on paper, an occupied town. Is anyone here nearly comfortable in the familiar body?

Rain nails us in, it has an insistent method, it hammers the tin that protects us. Each year lays a stone in front of the window, you come to understand how darkness explains itself only by expanding. Look into the coffee-black eye of a wolf, and there we are, innumerable limbs waving and gesturing, brilliant heads rolling in the animal dark.

# Heart

Poetry is a hard science of aloneness. It includes my girlfriend of five years trying to steal my expensive new coat in a dream. She's street-issue, a bedraggled nest of a girl, swollen and booze-weary, and has sloughed off her Salvation Army rag for Joseph's Technicolor dreamwear. Poetry, a kind of murder, which you will discover on your own. I command her to take off my robe, she undoes a slow button. It's butter. When she breaks for the door, I've got my hand fisting her hair, crushing a robin-blue egg in the nest. It all comes down to a pair of scissors wielded for my throat, the daytime sisters we keep in our kitchen drawer.

I'm going to fight for the coat, to the death of someone. I awake to the heart she has flourished on the back of a disabled poem. Wish of love and a day of words, the thunderstorms came quickly. Have borrowed the Korean War jacket, survivor from your father's signature in the great book of nightmares.

# Superman

Here's the scene, the second half of an evening,

my brother-in-law passed out on his bed,
my niece shaking him: *Dad, your father is dying.*

Nothing doing, you can't shake a large man free, floating on that sea of booze.

Finally, two pennies on his eyes, his dad Charlie had become a thing.

The first half of the evening, my brother-in-law telling a long tale of sexual exploit,
the usual mythic: forty days of rain, intercourse sixteen times daily,

a woman who was blonde all over

and disappeared pregnant one October night.

My brother-in-law bathing in a tub, literally, he claimed to have filled with his tears.

Superchild. Seeking you. Hoping you will be kind.

# Death of a Thing

It is a movement, a flow.

Some are fortunate. To be discovered, weeping in public.

Gasping for breath, you are now leaving the beautiful lake.

In the sand, on the red bridge, in the pebbles.

The sun, the gleaming fish.

Everyone wants a map, one of three stories to choose.

X marks the spot, where the fire is built,
X the place, where an ax used its tongue on the face of a tree.

There is no X,
no battered sign, on a road in a place called Vermont.

A new memory, that is without a mark. No enemy. And not this music.

The exquisite thing, shattering the surface.

It would be easier, if it died. But it does not die. It does not.

# Part Two

# Dickinson

*"Whom my Dog understood could not elude others."*

Thank you for the Embrace, my Tender Botany. I write that I might find you Pastoral, that we share the same Sky. Yet which the Vine and which the Tree, I cannot say. Nor do I doubt that you are Urban. Gathering the bones of Loved Ones, this is how Poets recite verses. Sharing your Terror, since September, I can tell no one, so I sing, as the Boy does by the Burying Ground, because I am afraid. Many say Lord Lord, then it comes Time to rip at the Carcass. When you open the Icebox, remember Me, my head among the Cabbages. My world, blue ice on cheap racks, only a Moment of Brilliance when You lean in. To say I love you includes many paragraphs, Of Course would be the Category. Is a bird Cryptic? We miss her point. Feathers and wings constellate around the beak, Face flat in the road viewed from Father's wagon. An Artist goes back for the Plastic Smile, an Eye. I have no doubt, I will be Killed by Toys. But Not to Cry for the wrong reason. There is such a thing.

# Astronaut Family

You will remember how Anne Sexton dedicated her life,
her rocket breaking up in the atmosphere.

Picture Sappho on a body of water she made with her tears.

Volition shoves the small boat toward danger.

Imagine Charlie Parker, committed to a science,
whose celebrity did not set him down safely.

The way, at the end of her life, Billie Holiday still whispered to us,
and was committed to her small dog.

Police and firefighters are heroes,

and, outside my window, the man throwing trash into the back of the
    steaming truck.

He operates levers, watches a girl saunter home. He risks losing an arm

to keep us from being up to our necks in eggshells and animal bones.

I speak, a man drops food or a bomb down to a foreign city,
each of us becoming the stars.

Brave explorers, who will praise us?

# Box for a Voice

In a box two or three away from this one, another song is playing.

Imprisoned in my radio, a chorus of voices from fifty years ago.

An old wooden shoe hangs on the wall, someone wore it, another painted it.

They ate grapes in the evening, heat laid them out on the floor,
not touching, their arms away from their sides,

in black and white on a chessboard called *then*.
The couple share fitful sleep, in a room with hot flies on the ceiling.

Ants come and go, their ancient gospel, to sleep by day in the floorboards.

Attempting to discover angles from which one might eat light and survive,
you and I,

undaunted moths.

# Forever Lyric

This field I lie down in has one religion, a belief in waiting in the dark.

Soon you arrive.

This year's plants fall, next year will be our best.

The emptiness calls me to take its place.

The shoes left outside my door are a bit narrow, but the length is right.

One day I'll fall, not exactly like the great maple behind the house.

I hope to go with the peace my spoons have in their kitchen drawer, cradling,

I hope you don't have the death of the knife.

I see us as people on a shore, wind in our hair, each of us holding our small bowl up to the waves.

# Snowball, with Policeman

I throw a snowball in a dream, it rolls past a policeman,

he turns around to face me, I wave, and begin to run toward him

(*at* him, he sees), his intense stare locked onto my smile.

The snowball is the only snow, behind him on the black tar.

He is standing where the double yellow line would be, but there is no yellow line,

only the iridescent trail of light the snowball leaves on the tar.

The light runs alongside me, alongside him, and beyond.
There is no need to reach for the gun—

his face is plenty—and we are frozen into the frame,

the sequence: me throwing the snowball,

his sudden, inevitable appearance turning toward my smile,

and the one simple, disturbing beauty

that is the light that runs parallel and will not touch.

# The Man I Love

The man I love changed his place in the sentence.

We lay out his body on this river of second chances.

A girl who could not find her way out of the paragraph,
she drinks the river again.

And Mother gone to fetch her, a perfect imitation of a stone.

That the priest would not even look at the altar boy,
the boy not do the same to his cousin,

we had our hopes.

Sometimes Why is simply a lament.

# Questioning Human Flight

Consider Jesus raised by men, hung in a tree with his arms spread,
and all quiet when he came down.

You fish Icarus from deeper in the envelope, packed in the cotton of myth.

1940s' German propaganda, swimmers leave the diving board behind,

some stay in the sky, Olympian on black and white film,
some come down to fly underwater.

The Germans in that age, even their eyes seemed to fly.

Then we adorned Dresden with fire,
a fancy frock coat, retributive justice, the collar buttoned tight to the neck.

We ask: useful, necessary, fun?

a rocket to the moon, a missile with people inside.

And one-way flight, suicide, homicide, the human animal
tumbling from a building, down the elevator shaft.

No.

Flight, to be flight, must not last forever.

# The Diners

I had three small children, with a side order of handguns.

Dolly had the salad of people dancing on her face,
the uncle who forced himself on her in the shower.

For the table to share, the family who would never believe.

No one to ask now that Father has gone.

A man is falling, a scream playing in the background.

There is one empty chair.

# Darkness,

Early on, this became a pattern,

you behind, me fleeing toward the light.

When I moved into young adult darkness, I would turn quickly,

trying to surprise you, trying to sneak up on me,
where else but in your temple of dark?

I have turned the tables on you,
I begin to enter you willingly.

A child casts a large shadow.

I search the city of my blood.

# Suicide

A coup has risen up, you suppress it.

You are the nation and the people who attack it.

You become your own security council.

You try then sentence yourself to hard labor. You catch yourself escaping.
While awaiting transport, you rape yourself.

You as probation officer look in on you the criminal,
you the judge tell you to go and live free.

You have a big party, invite all of you,

and awake the next morning with you,

someone you know who continues to surprise you.

You've begun to enter the body, and now there's no taking it back.

Razor, pills, the beautiful bridge. What matter that the gun isn't fired
so long as it was held with conviction in the mouth?

This moon waxes toward love, back again toward hate.

Your skin is a triple coupon, you cut it from your body.

The wake brings out quite the crowd of strangers.

No one who knew you remains to mourn.

# Physicians

The catalpa tree, the one with the large seed pods—they made me fear snakes.

Not one would rise to be a serpent, but the boy becomes a man.

Things take root, deep in the body, however namelessly.

No time to explain, she had to run. People escape us,
even the most loving embrace.

Do you know anything about loving? Doesn't love have anything to do with staying?

Shadow, I'll hold the light. You move the scalpel.

# Dialogia

I would like to be quoted sometime.

We get quoted, nearly.

We repeat ourselves.

To repeat, the essence of a good quote.

To be repeated by someone else.

Between you and me, there's a crowd on this platform.

The blind, they know tons about crowded rooms.

Know the thickness of draperies, simply by walking into a bedroom.

Can a blind person tell you about the cup? Half full, half empty.

It's a porcelain teacup, the table an immense field with hands.

And thinking, is it a quote if no one speaks it?

The spoon is in the teacup.

There's an old music, quoting itself.

The sun quotes itself, as do farms.

The moon is a paraphrase.

Each star an unprecedented scream.

# Creature

One-tenth the size of my deep, reflective pupil.

You who survived the cat and the broom. All black.

From the refrigerator, to the sliding doors of the balcony.

Walking the way the plants are leaning, seeking light, a way out.
Fleeing from, hurrying toward.

Wanting to pin my reasons on you.

The spider hanging behind us, the flower up ahead.

Singing for a mate. Eating your dinner. Pausing to weep. Maybe already dead.

Some would say I've wasted my life.

# Anointed

I once loved a dog so much, only when he stopped speaking
could I put him in the ground.

Bowl after bowl of goldfish too, with their lovely fan tails.

Convinced by their suffering, I began to collect stones.

The loneliest one I ever knew I desecrated
with a phone number, we were fourteen, and she never returned

my one courageous phone call.

One glass of water she threw in my face.
How many individual drops of rain.

# Crying Child

Let me help with that baby, lean into my language for awhile.

Already it's the second line. Call me Uncle.

Remember our early misunderstandings?
episodes of friendly fire, the prosecution we survived,

your cousin's head in the basket of grapes.

I won't ask you to forget forever.

The charter we signed gave you rights to pick figs in your own orchard.

The press was unfriendly to us. We were strong, young and ready,
and it cost us plenty to rebuild your village.

You said: *Mercy.*

After all we've been through.

# Part Three

# Note to All Concerned

On the shore, the moon breaks on the rocks, gathering and shattering itself.

The man admits surprise, how easily the point enters the heart.

You have only the one day, it's a birthday.
You can smile, I am, he did.

He buried iron pots and the cast iron pan, he washed them,
covered their surfaces with oil,

his face erased with the first shovel of dirt.

It was that cash register sound, something exact, a need.

He washed and dried his shirts, hung them near the invincible wall,
colors separate from the whites.

Curious, the whites were burning first, faster.

You too could enjoy the smell of your own car running in the garage,

semen on a towel.

One thing at a time now. Neurons being sent to the mailbox.

The word *stubborn*, having a wild time in his mouth. *Weary* on his lips.

Three trees he took down behind the house, he felt no need to assign
human and animal forms to the clouds.

The one thing he left reaching from the spinning earth, a poplar out front.

The white tongue was nailed there.

# Poem in Search of a Brother

I once rode a speeding bullet.

A Zen art to this. While riding, you must forget the bullet.

There is no bullet, no must, no you.

Central to the art, your nudity.
Beyond being naked, your breathing face,

which, while you sleep, is a screaming, silent moon.

My brother Matthew, never to appear in this dream or another,

this poem, this day, this fever.

Was he the force that propelled me? the target? the audience?
while dreaming me watched me on the bullet, sensing him?

Matthew, I want to save. Somehow, I must kill you first.

# The Grape

A man I know went to stay at a monastery.

While there, they taught him to eat one grape.

What's that like? I asked.

He was silent through the rest of supper,
then fell asleep on my sofa, which I thought was rude.

Years later on television, he set himself on fire at a demonstration.

To demonstrate what?

I eat the one grape,

I feel like I've been left alone in a really big house.

# Field in July

In the heart of a baby, somewhere in the long cord of the story that brings life, is the idea of a baby's shoe set in bronze.

Like the complaint of my partner's pants being too tight because of the weight she's gained since we fell in love, a single-engine plane passes like a soul over the backyard where we trim bushes and attract the season's hornets.

From a jar of roasted red peppers smashed at the foot of the glowing refrigerator, I pluck a tiny shard of daylight from her sensitive eyelid.

She is passion and gratitude, eyes so green that they become a field in July.

A baby crawls in search of a saxophone, weeds the height of my reader's heart.

You inquire as to the whereabouts of the child's mother.

The father is where he belongs: behind a tie in your mind, a paradigm hugging the telephone to his shoulder.

Set the story a hundred years ago, and both the parents are dead.

The shoe is in the attic, and still the baby crawls on in sunlight, timeless as the green metaphor.

Who knows whatever the baby will play when she reaches the attractive instrument.

# The Murderer, the Murdered, and Me

Now is always the season,

a man raising his shoe, a shovel,

a woman turning her head, lifting her hands, running from a room, or asleep.
The future doesn't care.

They were there, she no longer is.

Something implacable struck her, larger than his hands. History, time,
a shift between continents.

Arriving with a large boot print across the body of the envelope,
from his cell and my studio, these awkward, boyish letters.

A staple through each page he sends, as if they could incarcerate his words.

And what permanent weather, you know, for the woman in her box.

Running all my corridors, headed toward my door,
a torn blouse.

Biting the air, chasing, a man who would be my friend, his shovel raised.

Surely the door is bolted,
the men with the cage soon to reach my friend.

What. And to whom. I swear. I promise.

# December 2002 Letter to My Friends

If in the middle of the poem we have to move to another village, I'll expect you to lift your end of the sofa.

Hans W. Held taught me comparative politics at Jersey City State College.

All is calm, all is bright.

I am eating red chard and thinking of Anne Frank, Doctor's orders.

A) to eat the chard? b) to think of Anne Frank? c) to think of Anne Frank while eating the chard?

If you answered d), you would be correct.

That's enough. An inch to the left, or you'll knock over my aloe plant.

As a young man, Hans was a National Socialist, a patriot, and German tank commander during World War II.

"Chard," the doctor told me, "to address the constipation and the anemia."

"If you had a shop to run," he added, "you'd take an anti-depressant as well."

Something has gone wrong in the hippocampus, I jump but cannot remember.

I swear by the aloe, it has promising viscosity, and has escorted me through more than one gash or scrape.

Who can remember *how*? *Why* is always an option.

I admit it: the business about the shop made me think of Anne Frank.

With no shop to run, Anne lounged and wrote in her diary: "Dear Kitty."

Hans stopped at a Russian peasant mother's house, had his troops bathe and rest. It was war, he took for his men what they needed. As compensation, he left for the mother and her kids a case of German chocolate.

Careful. If you punch a hole in the ceiling, I'll lose my security.

Pardon me. That was my friend Regina on the telephone. She's 72, was born in Poland. She had to move quickly in 1938, and emigrated, despite some of her family choosing never to leave Europe. For Regina as a child, it was a big adventure. She converted, and as a young woman, met a man at the coffee hour of First Congregational Church. He was a sailor. They married and sailed. 33 years later he died of cancer. Regina and I have been friends for two years. Who said friendship is easy?

Russian troops come next, they find German chocolate wrappers in the woman's trash.

The couch won't fit in the room where I'm moving, I'm happy to have you take it.

Wanting to know where the Germans had gone, they torture to death her two young sons.

Something you whistle can keep you alive. Ask the children. You live with more suffering than you could've dreamed.

They get no information, they murder the woman for being a German sympathizer.

"Boiled lettuce" is a phrase that comes to mind. I wonder if it was "cabbage" in the original?

In the early editions of *Diary*, Otto Frank has his daughter's sex experiences removed.

I'm looking forward to the new edition. Aren't you?

No King or landlord in sight, there is snow.

From above, identify the round heads on the immense chessboard.

We move on black ice in the middle of a holy night.

# Billy Should Have Swum Toward the Raft

But Billy doesn't want to swim toward the raft, or he doesn't hear the voices calling.

What began as a joke or obstinacy,

what was adolescence and its momentary defiance of motherhood,

the categories of Oh whatever and Oh dear God
draw Billy out to sea.

Meanwhile a man on his way home to his wife falls into a pit
on the same street where he vowed never to again.

Under his jacket are brown eggs, a loaf of bread beneath his arm,

along with what's left of a bottle tied by a rope and swinging as it hangs over his back.

On his back in the pit, he imagines apology, forgiveness,

crushed eggs wet against his ribs,
the idea of his wife's lactating breasts.

What good will it do to know that his back is broken and he will never be forgiven?

Fantasy and truth are wings on the one bird. He is the happy and good husband.

Grounded. Billy's allowance will be docked. That's what the last look of terror is for: having to face the anger and disappointment of his mom.

They'll fish out his small goldfish body later. His mother will scream on television.

First he must drink what he can of the sea.

# Night in Haydenville

A large steel knife hovers above Main Street.

All night it goes house to house, poking its glowing eye through each roof in its turn.

It looks in on the accountant, sleeping fingers tabulating debt on a quilt.

The chief of police is safely asleep with his secretary. It was never about love.

Grandmother's in the basement beneath black cotton and a silver cross, in her mouth some prayer or curse in Italian.

Mother, against late spring and her fears, is up sealing the windows with gray tape and plastic.

A somnambulant runs with a blue guitar toward the bell tower.

There in the churchyard is the soldier who always loses at cards.

The curious knife follows our man with the blue guitar.

# The Room

The day is on its knees in the room. Nothing one can say or do to console it.

Peace and darkness, together in the one room. Not a very large room. They swim each other.

There are four people in the bedroom. The red-haired girl looks out the window. The three of them can go fuck themselves. See if she cares.

The furniture in the room was covered with sheets, for a very long time. Then three children priests made a candle offering to the night.

On the table in the north-facing art room, a note, with obvious signs that the person is gone. One possibility is to fold the note unread, put it in one's pocket, and carry it that way forever.

Who let in the moths? What is their place in history? Who among us has not thought of the moon as cheese?

Music. The room is not a stranger to music.

# More Questions for Study

Wine after poetry, beer behind the gas station, just home from an office party,

under the double circle of the fluorescent light, on the kitchen table, where it's your place for cereal, you see a single breast on a platter.

Do you a) invite your officemates over? b) put it by your mother's door with a note? or c) hide it beneath your coat and sneak it up to your room?

Once in your room, you try the usual whispering. The platter, on your work table, beside your last exam booklet. A good grade, but not excellent.

Was it wisdom or instinct, not to put the platter with the breast on your bed?

Does it matter that Grandma made the quilt?

Why did you remove the pencil and the ruler from the work table?

Explain, too, considering taping the breast to the platter and the platter to the table, then deciding against it.

The decision against sleep we understand, examining your jacket, carefully, before putting it back on.

Looking at the breast, in a way you've never seen one before,

implicated in a violence?

Do you cover the breast or leap out the window when there is a knock at the door? (Assume a second-floor bedroom.)

Yet there is no knock, you on the edge of the bed, the thing on the table.

Tell me the worst: A rape you pride yourself in surviving? The fact that you didn't grow up to be your bastard father?

The shoeless man, who undid his utility belt, before he tipped from the warehouse roof?

The night, in longevity, it has that evergreen quality.

There's a large white horse in the backyard, the floodlights pop on.

Across the way with binoculars, an old neighbor is watching.

# The Unintentional Thief

Remembering the story of the heart beating beneath the floorboards—

it gave away a murderer—the man who found the money,

throwing down the sewer the wallet he already swore was never there,
stuffed one-hundred dollars into the pocket of a tuxedo in his closet,

reminding him of the divorce, another hundred in his running shoes,
some metaphor,

and forty-seven dollars on the table
where he always put his keys

along with the money he'd budgeted for the week,

and with his heart hammering like the police, the face of a close friend
in his mind looking over his shoulder, he sat down and wrote

this simple poem, remorse and apology.

# Walker

She has to leave me, an appointment in a large field of what-not.

Where the woods begin, a cardinal in a tree, the ticking before the explosion.

Four people sit at a table, nod their heads *Yes*, life support and oxygen tent, they are the loving committee inside her head.

*A person isn't a plant, sometimes you fly or roll, even dawn goes at full daylight.*

*Police shoot raccoons at noon.*

*A moose has no business downtown in traffic.*

*Let him remain handcuffed to the tree, it's his fruit.*

Rattling jaws, I'm the car on a steep hill, held together by glue and gray tape.

Before you go, it's Wednesday, they're throwing the newspaper against the door.

Let me dress. I want to listen while you walk down the stairs.

# Remnant

Always a stain. Scarred leg of furniture.

The broken band. An elastic. Rarely the ticking watch.
The cliché on a white towel.

Teapot. Vase. The nest begun in a hairbrush.

The chocolate foil. Fingernails. Beneath the balls of early letters.

The thud, in sunshine. When a particular bird mistook the window.

The eyes mistaken.

Something rotten. Boiling in the heart.

Roadblocks. Numerous soldiers. At each checkpoint of the body.

# Toyland

A baby is crying in my mind.

A stone is falling behind my eyes, a dog is tugging
on the chain around my heart.

Boulders of speech, paragraphs. Complex, dependent clauses.

The small house of nerves is on fire.

One red ant and one black
trapped beneath a drinking glass. A man trembles above them.

At his back, a woman throwing words,

a crimson scarf bleeding from her shoulders.

His hands a pair of beautiful fossils, seated on his knees,
the right occasionally breaking the knuckles on the left.

The cat leaps, a bird is ticking in the great pyramids of her ears.

In many versions of the old story, they put a pillow over the child's face.

# The Lost Sock Being the One You Need

No goldfish of mine ever died because of a girl.

The number itself is only a den of thieves in the minds of men.

The cardinality of my family was nine.

Ordinally, the sixth was violently killed.

He wouldn't hurt a goldfish, my bishop of conscience says.

Still he could not save a beloved brother from murder.

Story: a boy takes his father's gun out to the field. He's four, the three-pound gun a twentieth of his weight. He enjoys the metallic-acid smell, another kind of blossom, while he tinkles on the gun in the weeds. He follows a spider as it scampers for cover. Twenty minutes later (this is not a math problem, perhaps not even ethical), he returns for the nearly forgotten gun, walking across the field and toward the barn with what an observer would call clarity or determination. There is no observer. Even you, who would have cared. Now is not then. But we must not be too hard on ourselves. Inside the boy's head, a movement that echoes the flight of the spider toward freedom. At the barn with one lucky shot, the boy drops his father's horse.

My father has yet to return Home from all his years of work.

When he does, he'll find that something he loves is missing.

# Hatfield

A man with two first names is cleaning his rifles,

always there is a dog barking,

shadows without a god, a helicopter, motives to fill a notebook.

Beside the highway, a number of pink men against a brown field, they punch the ground with Grandfather's tools,

a town raised beneath a fingernail.

Challenging the levee, the river is rallying,

Jacob's shack already leveled.

Men behind sandbags, every boy who knows enough to punch or spit, some of the older women,

we fire when the river shows its first white tooth.

# You Be Time, I'll Be Fire

Let x stand for all the things that we do together.

Hence we can proceed as follows:

Jimi Hendrix lights his hair on fire on stage in a club in the east Village.

My future brother-in-law hotwires a motorcycle. With his best friend Ray on the back, he rides into the front door of the club where Hendrix has lit his hair on fire.

Ignition when the two wires spark, flash when Hendrix lights his hair,

pop of bulb when the lucky photographer connects on this subset of existence.

Prove that the square of no rational number is unique to your family alone.

The next set should be fairly evident by now:

Ordinary things done in an unordinary way can produce unordinary results.

Add poverty to time, and some strange shit happens.

Let a stand for Hendrix singing "Red House over Yonder."

Let b stand for my future brother-in-law shooting two men in Viet Nam.

If b, then c: my brother-in-law gets a month off in the USA, Jersey City.

If a and c, assume d, a white, 1967 Corvette with windows steamed,

my brother-in-law-to-be and my oldest sister making e, my niece Stephanie,

while Hendrix on an 8-track tape plays with his teeth on his guitar,

the rock-and-roll symbol for his very own penis.

The alert reader will no doubt observe ways of simplifying certain parts of the equation by judicious manipulations of the system.

# Fire

I'm like you. I consume myself as I go,

content to contain myself, ready for entertainment,

entirely comfortable in the poet's red chair,

on a building, like a party dress, I can paint the whole town.

My work begins in a corner; my desire, curtains and pork.

Citizens volunteer to kill me in small towns,

some make pasta and play cards, wash their trucks while they wait.

The rush is to see me, to bathe me, I am the rage,

they pluck babies out of me, I am a very great mother

giving birth to heroes and orphans.

You don't have to go to the history of Rome,

no, Dresden was an example of me clapping my wings once.

You will come to see that I am the meaning in everything,

and that it was all up with me once I tasted hair.

I am not a joke, I visited early, I was there

in the caves, I helped humankind to matriculate,

tugging the dormant seeds of trees out of the earth and toward me.

I smiled on early straw huts and wooden cabins, settlers sang beside me

roaring their truth and sucking pipes of tobacco.

I split the atom and fed you napalm in return,

in the south, I loved your wooden crosses.

I am the single cause of jazz and the blues.

No manuscript lasts without me.

# A Song

A hundred-seventy human pounds, equal to one leaf late in autumn?

Other than the obvious, what's the color of death?

When no one sees the tree fall, could it be we all hear it forever?

Something the dog alone knows outside the door, for which he is praised or beaten?

When someone falls to his death, does he ever land?

Quietly flying throughout the day, screaming only while we try to sleep?

A song, a mothering we have yet to let go of?

Is it time for our lesson, a pledge, a secret handshake in a container of time?

Bug in a jar?

Light in one's hands cupped under the faucet?

The face reflected there thrown onto the face?

# Poem (Delicate Furniture)

Delicate furniture that is a man, delicate window of hope into a day.

I take my accomplishment of having awakened, of having accomplished sleep for consecutive hours,

I take my one broken shoe and my one good one, I place them on the sidewalk, they carry me among many faces.

Some faces are insult, others sanctity, I'm only talking about the ones inside myself.

Bodies on the sidewalk are nothing but angels, each carries a scroll, each reads from the divine plan of vulnerability.

I insect my way among the insects.

In my wallet, a signed photo of Bob Dylan, I signed it myself, a look more of disdain than concern, who knows what he was thinking.

I am thinking that the sun is a mother if you are wealthy,

and how the sun can be a total bitch.

Flood, Fire and Drought, Quakes, War, Disease.

I am thinking that the five books of the new century have yet to be written.

# The Lawn

*Using rational numbers, find the solution to this work problem.*

Kent can mow the lawn alone in 3 hours.

David can mow the lawn alone in 4 hours.

Find the time it takes the two boys to mow the lawn together.

It depends. Have the boys been drinking beer?

After the first hour of drinking and mowing, factor in (subtract) two minutes each additional hour for the boys to piss behind Mrs. Willoughby's rhododendrons.

If it's Saturday, Mrs. Willoughby will be home alone. What effect will this have on her psyche?

Consider that her deceased husband relieved himself, when mowing, in the same fashion.

If Mrs. Willoughby begins to weep and is overheard by Kent and David, will they knock at her door to check on her well-being?

Do we recommend that they knock together,

and how to respond if Mrs. Willoughby invites them in for lemonade or tea?

What if she's in her nightgown and the weeping was a ploy? All along she's lusted after our two young math students.

With one on each side of the sofa, she plies them with bourbon and water.

Your first error in calculation was to assume Mrs. Willoughby, perhaps elderly, is also lust-free—

the fallacy of elders not having active sex lives, memories of a firm thigh?

Assume now that the boys dislike bourbon, and being adolescents, probably don't need much plying to have sex.

Each blows his load without unbuttoning his pants.

Four, maybe five, minutes at most. They can't wait to get back to the lawn, sure as they'd be that their parents or the police are about to break in the door.

Under these conditions, they'll finish the lawn in record-breaking time.

Add back the minutes you subtracted earlier, deduct an additional minute or two.

But wait. Mrs. Willoughby's car's not in the driveway. She's gone to see Dr. McGovern, something about a suspicious spot the tests revealed in her upper colon. With nearly two-hundred feet of intestine, this could take time, especially since Dr. McGovern's been having an affair with his receptionist, and, as luck would have it, only yesterday his duplicity was discovered by his wife. Mrs. McGovern's outburst, understandable but shameful even to herself, lasted 7 minutes in the outer office, pushing all the appointments behind for the week, so Mrs. Willoughby *definitely* ain't back to see the boys mow the lawn. She hates not to be there while they work. She's both angry and excited that they relieve themselves behind her bushes. Today, however, she's mostly frightened about the spot in her colon, which is either more than *one* spot, or it moves. Or Dr. McGovern's a shoemaker and not a surgeon, and all his diplomas are fakes. Mrs. Willoughby wonders while she waits. She's considering a second opinion, but doesn't know whether her insurance will cover.

What relevance has this apparent digression to our boys mowing the lawn?

Kent. Kent is Kent McGovern. Oh my God. This poor mamma's boy happened to be in his mother's car on his way to ballet, when together they stopped, "for a quick sec," to say hello to his dad, and there his mother caught the two of them, that Sheila bitch receptionist smiling, in each other's arms. Kent was in his tights. These heterosexual displays of affection disturb Kent as it is, but to stumble on it together with his

Mom, who's also his best friend—he went and puked in the parking lot. She yelled. And his pirouettes at ballet, well they just sucked.

Let us remember that it's summer. Both boys are sweating. Kent came out a month ago. David is the only friend who didn't bolt. Truth be told, he spends more time with Kent now. Not altruism or charity. Sure it's friendship, and a little something more. Yesterday when Kent was in his state about his breeder father and the receptionist, David had come over, and together, with popcorn and "Some Like It Hot," they huddled together under Grandma's quilt. Nothing happened, except for the little kinetic electric sparks that ran on the quilt when one or the other moved slightly, getting a little more comfortable, alone together in the blue light from the old black and white film.

Factor this in. The boys have pulled the pickup under the private shade of the trees. They've driven up to the edge, near the dilapidated garages, far from the road and anyone but a couple of stray cats. What happens is both rough and caring.

However long it takes, both Kent and David will remember this lawn.

# Euler Did Not Consider Case 2

(Swiss mathematician, 1707-1783)

He was in the study with his apple porridge and his theory.

*My dearest, 186,000 miles per second light travels from my candle to the page where I write to you.*

His Beatrice was at Madam Mooragain's salon, where the port seamstress coaxed and convinced her into one more gown.

Amelia, her lady in waiting, read aloud Count Euler's letter.

No danger of compromise, no chance that Euler would mention any body but those celestial.

Her breasts pushed further into view nicely. Madam Mooragain pulled.

She recollected the boating party, sixteen guests in all, Euler so proper,

silently staring at the oar as it dipped again and again into the lake, and he made his notations.

It had been different with the young Ahmstad the painter, who saw no lack of metaphor between the oar and the lake.

He too sketched notions in a pad, and on a separate gray day

rowed them alone further, the outer end of the peninsula, where he gave her syphilis.

Euler need not know until after, and the child would be raised well by nuns in Corsica.

My little niece, she would say, bringing the poor waif to live with them.

*Beloved, let us once more consider the simply supported rectangular plate.*

*Buckling occurs here with a semiwave, also in the longitudinal direction.*

She would no longer have to suffer her intended's long-distance lovemaking,

she could have the painter in for family portraits in the winter—oh how she would enjoy the irony!—

blame the disease on Euler's single adolescent indiscretion with alcohol and the brothel.

But could she go through with it, kiss that acne-scarred face?

Madam Mooragain pulled.

Yes, she thought in the looking glass, smiling above her beautiful bosom.

She had heard that a certain charming young hussar, Count R's son, had of late returned from the front.

She would enjoy herself tonight at the old Count's ball.

# Einstein

Einstein stares into the parking lot. The yellow crime light is a sun to the shy opossum as she walks along the fence at the border of the property. Love thy neighbor with the proper divisions. Einstein is looking for the title of it all. *A Perimeter for Opossum. The Story of My Triangle Teeth. Razorsharp.* Point of view is the house in which the story occurs. Einstein knew that. And he had to know that you can't teach it to everybody. Looking out, he understands the futility welded to positive change. It doesn't make him unhappy. Intelligent optimism sets aside a room for murder. The opossum walks into the night where trees will diminish, highways expand. One might say she is looking for the cars that will kill her descendents. First she must eat. She must search out and bear the intransigence of a mate. Einstein realizes how he himself had to go through all the forms of the animal kingdom, to fight and claw his way into the world. Out of Germany, too. Only to find in the trash a little scribbling God had done on an index card. Einstein likes to look out the window. In school, they expected great things from him. He published what he found.

# Passengers

After the shops had closed Tuesday, I was eating your evening face in the woods.

A bit adolescent, my therapist says, and yet he admires the energy.

Wednesday crawled into the back of your passenger van, and the birds sang.

We are passengers, aren't we darling?

And if you don't bleed at the end of the month, we'll ask the forthcoming child,

Are we not on a journey?

I stole two rolls from the warm bag outside the convenience store,

the falseness of laminated Main Street softened by the cool blush before dawn,

while inside a man of middle eastern descent, whom the town treats as if his face were a façade,

snoozed and did not see me on the four tiny black and white screens near the register.

The radio in the van announces promises and heroes, and the boys and girls who should be home experimenting with drugs or getting laid

pull down a statue in the square halfway across the world.

You refer to my sex as a fabulous blue guitar. We are lit by brake lights, a long line of cars like adults going somewhere.

I see that you are part gray cardboard, part chocolate. I part you in ways that you desire to be parted.

In the black of your eyes, you sport the face of a man who looks like me.

He wears no shirt, a pair of the tiniest hands at work on his chest.

He is breathing heavy, and soon he will melt in the rising sun.

# Acknowledgments

Poems from *Strong John and the Hands of Antiquity* appeared in these publications:

*American Literary Review*, "Toyland"

*Artful Dodge*, "Hatfield," "The Red Fox," "Remnant," "You Be Time, I'll Be Fire"

*Barrow Street*, "A Beige Scarf"

*BOMB*, "The Unintentional Thief"

*Boston Review*, "Yellow Balloon Rising"

*Chautauqua Literary Journal*, "Fire"

*Conduit*, "Design"

*CROWD*, "The Incident. The Picnic."

*Denver Quarterly*, "Billy Should Have Swum Toward the Raft," "Colors from the Attic," "Strong John and the Hands of Antiquity," "Look into My Eye," "The Lost Sock Being the One You Need," "Poem in Search of a Brother"

*Eleven Eleven*, "Community Oom," "Death by Baloney," "In 500 Words or Less," "Three Dresses Above Cripple Creek"

*Fence*, "Superman"

*LIT*, "Poem (It came out)," "Suicide"

*Open City*, "Walker"

*Ploughshares*, "Night in Haydenville," "Note to All Concerned"

*Seneca Review*, "December 2002 Letter to My Friends," "Hands"

*Sentence*, "Dickinson," "Heart," "Road Test," "The Submission," Will of God," "Wolf Prose"

*Sycamore Review*, "Before a Storm"

*The Virginia Quarterly Review*, The Murderer, the Murdered, and Me"

Other Work by Samana, under the name Edward Bartók-Baratta.

*Fox Has His Day: Tales and Poems from the Far, Far North* (Sámi Education Council, Norway, 1998)

*Deep in the Night of the Body* (Premiered Northampton Independent Film Festival, 2003)

*Old New York City Where I Lay My Head* (CD, Poems & Flute, with Bassist Dave Wertman & Others, 2006)

*Book for John* (Poems, hardcover limited edition, MotherJill Press, 2008)

*The Sanctuary* (Ongoing sculpture installation and temple, Northampton, 2000-Present)